Discover Kai Poetry

Peaceful Resolution

First Edition

~ Peaceful Resolution ~

Peaceful Resolution

info@guaranteedpaperpublishing.com

About Kai

Kai is multifaceted, ever redefining and diverse; smudging the lines, eliminating black and white hard edges and judgment, and delving into varied shades of gray.

I have gained some knowledge, suffered much pain, and am better for the wear. Some memories hit me with a force, or whisper softly in my ear, and I am inspired to record them. Other poems are simply fanciful imaginings, wistful and unapologetic.

Email her at:

kai@guaranteedpaperpublishing.com

Ophelia...

A Division of Guaranteed Paper Publishing

12138 Central Avenue

Suite #542

Mitchellville, MD 20721

ISBN# 978-0615738383

The text of this book is set in Garamond.

Summary: The intimate thoughts, experiences, impressions and emotions of an author.

Dedication

To my children, who tolerate my constant scribbling and note taking, while they try to climb all over me. May you one day read my writing and realize that Mommy is merely human, and, although flawed, she is sincere in her attempts, expressions and genuine love. I write so that when you are older and more mature, you will have a roadmap or a glimpse into who I am and what my life has been, which may better explain your decisions and pathways.

Love you forever,

Kai

Table of Contents

My Baby Girl

You are filled with a unique essence
you exude deep loves joy
your being rhythmically inspired and musically
imbued
I am simply amazed by your very existence

Baby girl, in my womb you twisted and turned
rocked to inner dimensions clear vibrations
molding your natural melody and
developing intellectual prowess
your internal beat and flow
so different yet so perfect

Now I watch you
dance and spin
bounce and hop
twirl and tumble
climb and fall
nod your head and close your young eyes
rocking to the precious savory personal tune
He has instilled within your spirit

Your phenomenal radiation
simply unspeakable

a pure cosmically manifested essence
you are my life

The 4th Kiss

That 1st kiss
so light and fresh
barely there, I almost missed it
never knew a boy's lips
could be so soft, so gentle

The 2nd kiss
awoke something in me,
snapped me out of
playful reverie
brought reality clearly into focus
paying more attention to the
here and now

The 3rd kiss
made me melt
my knees literally buckled
my head swooned, then
time stopped
My ears started ringing,
blocking out all sound
but the pounding of my heart

The 4th kiss

sealed the deal
making me completely yours
I woulda done anything you said
woulda followed you anywhere
in that moment
opening the gates and
freeing all of me
at your mere request

Thankfully,
you had no idea
of the power of
that 4th kiss

I Remember

I remember,
even when I don't want to
trying to move on
forget
erase it all
cause I'm grown now

Time moves forward and
thoughts of the past are
wasted current energy
randomly scattered on fixed events
stagnant and permanent
that can't be removed
or fixed

But yet, I still remember
dwell on it just a bit
fruitful, innocent love
pressed flat against corridor walls
under basement steps
behind open doors
molded into you
pressed onto me
learning desire and discovering

intimacy's natural reaction
both new, both scared
both surprised by such intense experiments

Yeah, I still remember

Sexy Back

You know, you brought me back
released me and inspired me
reunited me with womanhood and
all it's delightful secrets
reminded me of the little delicacies
contained within this feminine glory

I love being a woman

You know, you made me shine
skin glowing and sparkling
I feel my flow
stretch my hands out wide
and watch my colors spread out, percolate and
splurge
mixing and separating
a never ending waterfall of blessed hues

You know, you brought my sexy back
subtle smile at your suggested hints
tilted body leaning into your sway
maneuvering myself with feline prowess
enjoying flirtation, sliding cute phrases and
intimate encouragement your way

You know, you brought creativity to me
my mind stirring up lewd and luscious thoughts
unmentionable wants churning my pit into
somersaults
loosening tongue lingo in your presence
sliding written word prowess into your lap

You know you brought my sexy back

Silent Attempt

How did I feel to you
tell me
did you notice the softness of my body
the fullness of me
did you recognize my mounted pressure against
the lean swerve of you

Was it alien and foreign or
did I feel like home?

What could I have done
what should I have said
did the warmth of me send a clear signal
uninterrupted and static free?

Maybe I could've pressed harder
made sure my blossoms left a
carved imprint into your heart
or probably should have
opened my mouth and let it spill out
clarified my desired intent

but we both know
that is something I

would never do

So, did my message come across to you
were you able to properly decode it
translate my desperate meaning
for what it was worth?

or did my secret attempt to
reach you end up
misjudged, abandoned and unwanted?

So Easy

Had to hold it back
to stop and disengage from the possibility
of getting lost in you
tied up in you
releasing self to you
freeing self to you

Had to back it up
reel it in and
place the cover on
with a genuine smile and
light humor

This pulsating want so damned
distracting and disturbing
rendering clear thought impossible
forcing manipulation into
initial innocent intent

What do your arms feel like
how I long to be wrapped in between, endlessly
Twisted and turned,
disappointingly discarding
this rare opportunity

and distant moment of freedom
inevitably overrun by obligations clarity

Embarrassment replaced want
because it shouldn't be this way
it shouldn't be so open, so easy
so clear
But it is and I am

Still

I can still hear him
his voices carries in my head
hoarse and dry
thick with emotion and want
promising me forever
the sound moves me
breaks my resolve and
loosens the very core of my being

I can still feel him
lips pressed against the shell of my ear
moving slowly to the top of my neck
arms wrapped firmly around me
drawing me in
hands gently pressing and lightly stroking
pressed flat against the small of my belly
understanding the swell of my body
his simple touch and exploration
causing me to catch my breath and
close my eyes
bite my tongue and
ride his tidal wave

I can still taste him
lingering on each and every bud
his sweetness so addictive
overwhelming me
arousing an innate yearning hunger
an insatiable craving for him

I can wait
with my eyes closed, my body still
my mouth shut
I can wait
because I am still with him

I Musta Forgot

I musta forgot
sat up here and let go
let myself loose
released necessary inhibitions and
opened wide
uncorked the vacuum seal to my
scented essence
handing it over to you

What was I thinking
entrusting my most secret self
in your careless hands
my most intimate being given
to your arrogant person

True to your core you
took note, inventory, stock of
who I am and what matters to me
absorbed whispered secrets
during the height of intimacy
like an eager sponge that, with manic delight,
you now squeeze and wring
until the soft flesh
tears and rips

dripping poison
into these open festering wounds
etched into my skin like
swollen welts with each
disillusioned realization stinging like salt from
your tongue
hurled at me
aimed to destroy me

I shoulda known, but
I musta forgot

Simply Love

Love doesn't mean fulfillment
partnership or companionship
is not a cure for
loneliness' ache nor
provides long term relief
from depression's isolation

Love cannot compel understanding
comprehension
a sincere, deep seeded attempt to
to learn another soul
It does not give lessons
or provide guidance into
how you think, operate
there is no template or
instruction manual to decode your
secret needs

Love fails to extend
sincere appreciation or acknowledgement
belief in one without judgement
encouragement without envy

Love is simply love

pure joy and elation
dwelling within an empty vessel
until the pressure mounts and bursts
or subsides and slowly fades away

Love is simply love

Spirit

Want to feel the pure spirit
of this day
the promise of
universal peace and true uninhibited love
kindness
so very necessary
like a cool patch against
raw skin
chaffed by the hardness, coldness
dismissiveness
of this world

I believe that it can be.

Yes, it is possible
tonight I can focus on the
special promise of salvation's birth
and tomorrow
reflect and celebrate
believe and rejoice
dismiss my fears and doubts
drown out my disappointments and pain
press pause on my personal pity party
and extend myself to the

promise of
this day

Despite it all
I sincerely believe in the
Spirit

Broken Dreams

Do you really and truly believe
that I am the cause of your problems
that my decisions broke your dreams
my requests erased your future?

How did the years of support
backbreaking loyalty and love
become so easily dismissed
so lightly forgotten

You don't recall the wars fought on your behalf
me against the world,
while you sat on the sidelines to
Me choosing you and yours
over my own life
my own freedom
my own dreams, gifts and talents

I built with you
worked with you
listened to you
encouraged you
for years

while you made excuses
how enough wasn't enough
how your focus had changed
how the dream just wasn't in you
Now in hind sight, it's my fault?

Maybe it is
Cause I gave away too much
waiting for an even exchange, eventually
instead your support takes on envious form
judgmental and angry
my need dismissed as self pity
my wants always weighed against your
coulda shoulda's

you know what
you see me like the world sees me
the gloss, the bullshit
the fake accomplishments that mean nothing
more
than another paper mounted on the wall

After a decade or more, you still haven't met me
learned me
taken the time to see me
understand me

Only to you, I tried to show my soul
opened it and laid it out
You slammed it shut
like a dry book
uninterested, bored, so desperately hoping
I'll just shut up, go away
leave you to this week's hobby
this month's new interest

You never know
you just may get your wish.

Sleeping With the Enemy

Whether in the same house
same room or
same bed
I have slept with the enemy
all my life

Lying on my side,
facing the door
keeping one eye open for
hallway light to cast that shadow
forewarn me of her imminent entry
through kicked door
my hand resting lightly on the
knife that permanently resided under pillow
through adolescent and teen years

Something always kept her back
insults and hate shouted at me
accusations more appropriate for a mate
or spouse
tossed my way
floated across air, messing up my head
but something, something

32

kept her from crossing that threshold and
laying hands on me
shaking and hitting, making me feel helpless
hopeless
like before I sought solution
in a weapon

I eventually escaped
able to finally sleep, rest
fully relax, my bedroom no longer
a fortress or stronghold for my
last stand and safety
and then you,
you brought peace and comfort
entered my tiny valley and poured in sunlight

Until life inevitably tested you
changed the variables forcing
growth and maturity
difficulty and indecision
Then I became the fault, the blame
the reason for failed ideas and broken dreams
despite the other obvious variables that
you still refuse to consider

So now I am back
to facing the door while

lying on one side
knife within easy reach, just in case
ensuring my protection
guarding my life for just one more day
through one more night
because I am once again
sleeping with the enemy

Nothing

As amazing as it seems
your anger no longer hurts
no longer tears at my heart or
rips into my being
I find myself oblivious to its
irrational release after
days, week, months of silence
minimal acknowledgement
sidelong judgmental glances and
unexplained disdain

We've done this dance
too many times before
and I know the signs like the
watching the change of the moon
can tell when you switch from
love to hate
support to disdain

It happens so often
so routinely
it feels like second nature

So we are back to hate, huh

yeah, I charted it, knew it was due soon
prepared myself and waited
for my pounding heart to hurt
the internal bleeding to pour through

But, while you
dispense verbal lashing
like liquid molten hate
I am discovering that
I feel absolutely
nothing

Forgiveness' Throne

Where is forgiveness
and why does he elude me
avoid me
try me with hopes of peace and
possible redemption, insinuating a resolution
for long desired completeness

Like a wild horse he
bucks me, throws me
I grasp with both hands,
desperately throttled and thrown
while forgiveness seeks to dethrone and deflate
challenging me for daring to rein him in
daring to tame him
foolishly trying to contain him

But I need forgiveness
on bended knee, I plead for him
cause he has giving me a taste, a hit
like the drug of a fiend
I want more, need more
can't bare the thought of life without him
willing to turn over every stone until
he is found

fight ever battle, until I die or
he succumbs

So many times I think I have him
sealed and suctioned
lured and steady and
knowing how to manipulate him
I attempt to ride him to my kingdom and
boast of my greatness because of him

But the truth is
forgiveness resides around my heart,
but not quite within it, and
try as I might
some things he simply has not given me
the key to accept nor
the plan to move on
the ability to swallow without responding
to recall without judging
so, for right now
while I desperately need what he chooses to keep
I am at his command

Slow Walk

We walked slowly
taking our time
kicking pebbles and laughing lightly
easily chattering, your teasing
making me laugh
smile despite myself
giving me thoughts to cherish
for the rest of my day

You sat next to me
class partner, complaint sharer
saving a seat whenever I
slid in too late
patting it, smiling
nodding for me to know
it was only for me

I passed you notes
whispered
leaned over while your
wild locks tickled my cheek
speaking so close to your earlobe
so close to you
smelling your masculine cologne and

wondering if you thought of me when you
sprayed it on and
tucked that beautiful mane under nappy cap
my thoughts escaping me
so busy observing you sitting still and smooth,
unmoving as the
light air left my mouth and
softly tickled your neck

We anticipated each other's expectations
enjoyed one another's mellow vibe
sought unity in the knowledge of
New York cool
confident expression of friendship
teeter tottering on
other possibilities, but
which one would be bold enough
to cross the line?

Not me, I took your
silent offering for granted
simplistically relying on your
modest presentation of nonchalance
ignoring the occasional spark, unsure of its cause
I remained silent, scared of love's possibility or
rejections likelihood

Not you, noticing my other friendships
other relationships, determining that the risk
seemed too great, the loss easier to save face
rumors of my raw man
too loud and the boy/girl
game simply too easy, cause too many
other girls always so accessible
always waiting in the cut
to get to know you

So we continued to walk, slowly
taking our time and
choosing two different paths.

Our House

If we continue to
bump these walls
shake this structure
shout and fight within its
damaged walls
our house will surely fall

If this anger doesn't subside
calm or dissipate
it will continue to rage
mount; engage, coercing you to
respond
feeding your seething hate
love crisscrossed
pure emotion misled
misguided
twisted and perverted
our house will surely fall

If we fail to mount this life
on the cornerstone of His might
it will miss the mark
slide sloppily down the walls of this union

dripping acid, burning through drywall and
foundations steel, and
our house will surely fall

If trust doesn't go past
the visible, apparent
and every interaction inspires
spite's reaction
we won't make it
we will manifest death, and
our house will surely fall.

Manness

Manness.

Wrapped in bittersweet
dark chocolate
stinging the roof of my mouth
activating eyes stinging
and mouth watering
longing for the
taste of you

Manness.
Wrapped in
luscious dark caramel
warmed by the
pure heat of my desire
molded between
these soft palms
pressed firm and thick
becoming
hard and solidified
as I breathe light
to cool the molten form
my breath sweet, released softly

against the statuesque state
like soft wind upon
your body
staring deeply
into your eyes
burning timbers of
future dream, future generations
golden life wrapped
within the core of us

You are deep.
A never-ending caramel well
bittersweet dark chocolate
swooning midnight gloss
releasing an everlasting
effervescent glow

Your inherent powerful vibration
stimulating my very being
keeping me forever
fixated upon you

Manness. Iridescent.
Manness.

Hide It

I tried to hide it
disguise or dismiss this
pounding want
locked in the pit of my chest
at center of my heart

I have to hide it
ignore it, pretend that the
deep searing burn
ignited by your intimate smile
is nothing but simple heart flutters
manifested by quickened pulse
completed unrelated
to you

I've decided to
keep it my secret
forever locked sealed in the
cedar chest buried under my
blanketed soul
behind the deepest depths of my
inner spirit
hoping it will fade

evaporate
Maybe one day I will see you
again
Maybe one day I will know you
again
Maybe one day I might touch you
again
Oh, please, can I just breathe you
again

No, I will hide it and
it will sizzle and vaporize
against the intense heat
of my pure want
and then maybe I will be released
finally
from the simple cursed
memory and desire
of you
love

I Am Malleable

Peeled back too many layers
soaked, then shaved away
one too many calluses
saturated the thick skin that
served as the
impenetrable barrier against my foes

Now I am soft
malleable
easily penetrated and visibly hurt
wounded
blood drawn from a prick of a pin
my core, smashed by
a single blow

In pursuit of peace
belief of happiness
I stepped away from my
protective cloak
letting it fall away
the shield that sustained the
parental attacks and inner city drama
those bricks that absorbed

physical jumpings and
hid me from
hates target practice

Now, nothing remains to
block that dagger
you so easily aimed
at my soul

Less than Average

Foolishly believed my life
would mean something
someday
Thought, when it was all said and done
that I would have mattered
made a difference
inspired and encouraged others

Hoped I might
at the very least
make honorable mention in this game
float along the hubris of
the cosmic energy
until the collective occasionally plucked me out
recalled and appreciated

But the reality is
I have failed to make even the slightest dent
strike an indelible mark,
haven't even splashed blood red
on this canvas of life

I have done nothing to

put me in the minds of the collective whole
encourage or stimulate my people
set an example of courage or tenacity

Yeah. When it is all said and done
I have come out less than average
and certainly no more than common
the supernatural mission
whispered in my ear at birth
has not been completed
the talented tools loosely held, easily discarded
misplaced, carelessly allowed to fade

In the final judgment
when the totality of my life is measured and
weighed
I'm afraid that I will be left wanting
I know that I have come up short...

Your Everything

Desperately needed to be
somebody's everything
somebody's someone
do I matter
to anybody?
at all?

Searching for validation
never obtained at home
never given without
qualification
exception or
selfish intent

Prayed for a mate
soulful and kind
protecting and true
seeing
seeing my real value
recognizing my internal beauty
realizing my special worth

Failed to notice

caring's kind reflection
in so many hopeful eyes
and thought myself
too unworthy
to even consider
more than friendship

Only you.
Only you made it past
my flawed internal filters
Sparking my interest and
Pulling at my heart

Only you made me
your everything.

Your Photo

Find myself still stunned
shocked
when I come across your photo
can't believe you were
ever
in my world

Bet you don't ever remember
the first time I saw you
checking in that Spanish themed motel
scared as hell about
future undergraduate success and
sad about high school familiarity
left behind

Saw you and all thought
stopped
ceased
past boyfriends disappeared
clear future canvas
awaiting your imprint

And our paths continued to cross

science bound themes
leading us together and then apart
like the rhythmic vibration of lust

And I repeatedly dropped the ball
unaware that you could even conceive
of what I felt
what I believed
what I wanted

Forever misconstruing direct attempts for no
more
than simple friendly conversations
to pass the time

But your photo
still creates an internal shock and
I linger on the thought or possibility
of us...

My Musician

My musician
finding beauty in the soft curl
of each note
connecting his heart to the
solid pound of each beat

In his eyes I see
intricate melodies,
lilting, tinkling, dancing lightly
over his steady baseline that
deeply vibrates
resonating with the very fiber
of my soul

Watching him create
mesmerizes me
I find myself stunned by the simple magic
created by his hand and the
full ensemble pouring forth
effortlessly while he
remains focused, oblivious
in tune only with his manifestations
the rhythm pouring directly from his spirit

~ Discover Kai ~

I smile, move, dance
distract him
headphones removed, volume increased
he comes to me while
his rhythmic masterpiece fills my ears
his fingers play a matching melody
finding staccato notes,
drumming up and down my body
and his body
catches the baseline
thundering its own groove
consuming all of me

Receive and Return

I remember when it happened
when love finally pushed open the door

yeah, I knew
although I didn't say
you were so secretive
hidden
tucking away your emotions
locking your heart in that
special vault

But that night
something felt different
special and lovely
gentleness oozed from your caressing fingertips
adoration poured from your darkened eyes

Your lips spoke Solomon's song
deep into the well of my ear
Your tongue sprang out
declarations of emotions before
searching and locating
its natural counterpart

You and I
so easy, so smooth
We were both surprised that
this felt so right

Yes, that night changed everything
while I stared at you and wondered
what happened
that melted the ancient glaciers
and broke through your supernaturally formed
dam

I discovered that you
had finally decided to
receive and return
my love

Attica

Have ever you been
on the inside
deep down in the wretched bowels
of our societies underbelly

Have you smelled the
raw stench
of rotting life
passing, wasting away, disintegrating into
reminiscing of a life
never given a chance for
clean living

You think you're a soldier, huh
Imagine your beautiful woman
visiting on that weekend bus
your sexy mamasita
applying makeup and pulling on stockings
in the dank dark bathroom
only to have unnamed guards
strip her, search her
rub treacherous hands all over
her body

degrading her very attempt
to be feminine, loving and supporting

Can you even begin to fathom the quiet but
thunderous moment when
the heavy barred door to
the world as we know it
clangs shut,
forever sealing her in with
the nation's most murderous, most treacherous
most vile and most cruel
In case of uproar her only hope for survival rests
on
a clear ink stamp
on the top of her hand
that the X-Ray machine might verify
belongs to a visitor;
if she makes it

Have you ever smelled the
nauseating stench of
grown men incarcerated
tasted the putrid hate of
lustful envious eyes
Tried to maintain ice cold calm
and still your beating heart
to stare down the

curious eyes of a terrifying human animal

Have you ever experienced Attica?

How Could He

Why can't I breathe
in his presence
quickly looking away when he
glances in my direction
wishing I could just
disappear, vanish
turn into a mere whisper
a faded memory
whenever I feel his gaze on me

He is so beautiful
breathtakingly gorgeous
an easy smile and magnetic eyes
firm hands, wide chest
I want to get lost in the curve of him
ride the smooth sway of him

But, he is too much for me
looks too good for me
what I am thinkin
he would never, could never
even consider me

I am forever stuck in friend zone

Not fly enough to be his
wouldn't be able to compare to
the many girls clawing for him
wouldn't be able to withstand
the nonstop insults slung at me
for even attempting
to think myself worthy

He thinks me clever, smart
cute, maybe funny
He finds reasons to grab me
touch my hand
hold me close
I luv the throb of him
can't wait for the vibe of him

But we always laugh
playfully flirt
as I pull away
retreat
inhale and pray
that I haven't made a fool of myself
that I haven't revealed my true heart
and set myself up for rejection

Cuz, I know he is too fine for me
doesn't really want me
I mean
how could he?

Limits to Love

There are limits to love
lines drawn in the sand
clear destinations and demanded clarifications
that we disguise and hide
or ignore and deny
until led to the brink of destruction

I love you completely
will do anything for you
anything to please you, satisfy you
hold you close and
keep you near
anything.
well, maybe

anything contains a natural limitation
an actual definition as
most things that won't violate
my standards of self respect
at least not to the lowest points
won't repulse my sensibilities
or take me so far into it's loving depths
that I am unable to pull myself out

unable to breath without
claustrophobic suffocation

Please, stop pushing, testing
draggin me closer and closer to my
unbreakable limits, toyin with love's death
like a moth to a flame or a
dead mouse dangled before a cat
so curious to determine whether my love for you
will lead me down destruction's path
will be so loyal to you that
I will blindly walk into the enemies throne

You will have to accept
that I love you,
will do anything for you, but
there are limits to my love

The Truth

This man has got me havin
flashbacks, urgent recalls
got me remembering
lovin and love making
its sweet effervescent
filling me like
compressed vapor, squeezed into
confined space, got me full
mentally full
stuffed, overloaded and uncomfortable
with anticipation rising intently
just from the remembering

oh, the memory

unbelievable what you do to me
15 years and still fresh, razor sharp
just focused anew
crisp like clean waters and
trickling, drip dropping, splattering against
bare skin, fingers wide open
hands and palms upturned
fully consumed, overflowing

grasping and clinging

my man is the truth

causing muscle memory to respond
to the sound of his voice over
cellular waves, yielding the same
bodily tremors at the suggestion
mere mention
of future promised engagement, slowly exhaling
to regain composure
mind filled with
sudden promise of
unity and separation
flash heat and cool chill
making music with this most
intimate instrument, this most
sensual vital vessel
reserved for his
personal playground

my man is the truth.

Found Your Groove

I can feel you now
it took a little while
I didn't understand, at first
couldn't quite catch your groove and
couldn't comprehend the scope of your flow
grasp your uniquely sublime rhythm

but I'm learning
figuring you out
studying and training in the
possible learning of you
taking my time to
discover and incorporate
change and adjust

please, stop smilin at me
while I explain this, your
making me blush, but I want you to watch
that smile of your is causing
reminiscing of dirty thoughts and
nasty things

pay attention, see how I've

found your vibration
fell in sync with your sure steps
swaying my hips to your
manly tune

Now you've stopped smiling,
you've finally noticed
that I have found your groove

Time to Wake Up

He came to me
in a dream last night
startling and surprising me, my heart raced
cause the previous attempts to recapture his
unique features and expressions always alluded
me
my mind choosing to release his perfect reflection
for sanity's sake

But there he stood, leaning over and looking in
while I peered through and reached up
a decade later, his sight still spurred magnified
charge
throughout every fiber of my soul

My body melted and mind yielded while
he stared intent but worried
committed to this chance, but bothered just the
same
I rubbed his cheek, persuaded him to
release fear, utilize this singular world
promise this one oasis of peace connecting the
mental interlude that would

remain between us two

He sighed and relented, finally indulging a
decade old desire, an unspoken yearning that we
both
ducked around and dodged
finally free to fully explore, want and touch
I laid my palms on his chest as he
lightly kissed my shoulder then
stared into my eyes
back arched as he lightly held the
wrapped his arms around the width of me
firmly, smiling so faintly, so certainly
relaxing and giving in

but, somewhere, someone called my name
while I held on with clenched fists and
forced concentration to remain, his burning eyes
filled with sadness, acceptance of impending
disconnect
but he held me tighter while the voices got louder
and louder
then he kissed me gently, exploring the whole of
me
one last chance, one last moment
but the pressure of his lips faded, then dissipated
as the image collapsed and I opened my eyes

while
children stood over me yelling
"Mommy, it's sunshine! Time to wake up!"

Descriptive Want

Scrumptious, the very sight of you
excites me, anticipation rises
expectations mount, I want a
nibble or just a
small taste
give me a little sample
a morsel to
roll around my tongue

Delicious, I find you
nicely delectable
can't get enough, got an
insatiable area only you can
satisfy, tender space only you
can fulfill
only your special touch
can calm

Wonderful, I think your
beautiful, sexy as hell
masculine and firm, the
small of your stomach
pulses beneath my touch
the tender swath of skin

upholds against my gentle press

Sensual, your hips feel
heavenly, press fitted against mine
secret hollow comforting
this private desire
tender moments while instinctively you
stare and seek
incredible fulfillment at the
soft velvet of my pinnacle

Luscious, your lips feel so
powerful and full
laid against the side of my waist
or along the inner ridge
of my thigh
applying moist distribution
of demonstrable love

Complete, you seem so
full to me, fine and confident
unified and whole
needing no one else
applying your attention
solely to me

New Threshold

That one look
a suggestive glance
three simple whispered words and
a gliding palm
inching every slowly
toward my precious temple

Concentration shattered
immediately reversing the decision
upheld morals and ideas dissipating
resistance steadily evaporating, fading
diminishing quickly leaving me open

Lips against my collar
causing heat to surge through my neck
pounding pulse, indicating
racing blood, rushing, swimming
creating slight headache and
gentle physical ache

Open lips
gasping for air
muttering your name

searching without abandon
needing to find their counterparts to
still the sudden urgent tingling
in the roof of my mouth

Causing shivers under your
very touch, warm breath
clouding my senses
opening the natural faucet of
desire and seduction
luring you and
welcoming your guided entry
yielding to this
new threshold of sensation....

I Will Not Share You

I will not share you
no, it is not an option
I will not watch while
you are enjoyed
spread out, taken in and
made thin
by the vultures that need to envelope
seek to consume
must embody your essence to
absorb your energy

You are mine
Simply
Fully
My love has marked you
identified you as
sacred to me, sacred to loves life

With me you will
understand exhilaration
release your precious seed
find solace in the folds of my being
receive stimulation for brilliance
unforeseen

With you I can relax my mind
give myself completely
understand the rhythm of our unity
and bloom under the watch of your
delicate eye

You are mine
and I will not share you
rather I will submerge myself in
the blessing of loving you

Don't Mind Waiting

I'm waiting for you, baby
glancing at the door whenever
there is a creak or sound
holding my breath
anticipating you

But, no, don't rush
I will gladly wait
Just the mere thought of you
leaves me full, complete
satisfied and sustained
able to hold on and
remain contained
until you return

You are worth the wait
so attentive, you have
studied my natural flow
chartered my rhythmic hum
determined the keys to play that
strike my sensual chords

Got me purring out
intimate melodies I never knew

flowed within
leaving me aching for your
intimate touch, firm grasp
detailed approach and
continuous climactic yield

My mind is already spinning.

So I'll wait
patiently
for your arrival.
Take your time, handle your business
when you are ready, prepared,
then please, baby
come to me

If Only

If only I could
let go and release
turn myself out
completely
allow my mind to
absorb all the possibilities
become agile and flexible
willing and yearning
for new experiences

If only I could
shut the door on
past mistakes and
create an eraser to
wipe memories away
pretend I didn't trip
hadn't fallen
laid splayed out on my back
for all to see

If only I could
recreate me
add in more courage
sprinkle in a bit of strength

a dose of forgiveness
a little bit of faith
belief that my
root won't eventually rot and
my cornerstone will not crack

If only I could
be sure
force myself to believe that
my foundation will not
eventually crumble

If only

Seeking Solace

Desperately
seeking solace in your smile
silence in your satisfaction
strength in your mesmerizing stare
sublime solidarity in your smugness

You are the
sunshine of my singular existence
simple soup for my splintered soul, a
salve on this painful sore, my
surreal sunflower in the midst of sorrow.

Temporarily Release

You represent freedom
an opening, a crack
the slight sliver in this plaster
a tiny hole in this foundation

I need to slide through
bend my body to
conform to your opening and
push in, bow down
fit within the seams
as best I can

It is my one opportunity for escape
Release
Sanity
Breathe

So I cling to you
grasp onto your moving form
clench to this one opportunity
the slight chance to
escape
exhale

submit
if only temporarily

Novels also at Novels by Kai

www.facebook.com/pages/Novels-by-Kai

www.twitter.com/authorkai

info@guaranteedpaperpublishing.com

www.guaranteedpaperpublishing.com

www.ingramcontent.com/pod-product-compliance
Lightning Source LLC
Chambersburg PA
CBHW070550030426
42337CB00016B/2435